The Best Message of All

A gospel presentation for kids

Sandy Baldwin

Illustrated by Gary Ferguson
Colored by Richard Erbacker

WestBow Press books may be ordered through booksellers or by contacting:

WestBow Press
A Division of Thomas Nelson & Zondervan
1663 Liberty Drive
Bloomington, IN 47403
www.westbowpress.com
844-714-3454

Illustrated by Gary Ferguson
Colored by Richard Erbacker

ISBN: 979-8-3850-1304-3 (sc)
ISBN: 979-8-3850-1305-0 (e)

Library of Congress Control Number: 2023922192

Print information available on the last page.

WestBow Press rev. date: 01/29/2024

WESTBOW
PRESS®
A DIVISION OF THOMAS NELSON
& ZONDERVAN

The Best Message of All

For God so loved the world, that he gave his only Son, that whoever believes in him should not perish but have eternal life. John 3:16 (ESV)

1

The Big Surprise

Do you know that God loves you and wants to be your friend? The one true God who made all of the universe... he knows all about you, he loves you and he has great things planned for your life. God is getting a special surprise ready for us. Do you know what it is? It's a wonderful place called heaven.

I wonder what heaven will be like. God's book, the Bible, tells us that there will be a beautiful city with a street of pure gold, walls made out of jewels, a river as clear as crystal and a tree that never stops giving fruit. There will be no darkness in heaven because God's light will always be shining.

He will wipe away every tear, and no one will be sad or sick or get hurt ever again. Everyone will be full of joy as they celebrate God's love. God's kingdom is more wonderful and exciting than anything on earth. He's inviting all of us to come and be with him someday. But there's something that keeps us away from God. Do you know what it is?

The Big Problem

Sin is what keeps us away from God. Sin means doing something that God says is wrong. Who are the people who have sinned? God's word says that all of us have sinned. We have all done, thought and said things that do not please God.

Even though we may try our hardest, we cannot get rid of our sin. Sin is like a huge, thick, unbreakable wall that stands in front of us. We are on one side and God is on the other. Many people try to get to God in their own way. But the wall of sin is too high, too wide and too deep for any of us to get past it. How can we ever come to God? Is there anyone who can break through and set us free?

The Big Rescue

The Bible says that there is only one way to God. Jesus said, "I am the door" and "I am the way, the truth, and the life. No one comes to the Father except through me." Jesus is the only one who can break through the wall and rescue us from our sin. Do you know Jesus?

13

Jesus is God's one and only Son. God sent him to earth as a little baby. Jesus came so that he could show us the way to God.

15

When Jesus grew up, he taught people about God and did many wonderful miracles. Jesus healed all of the sick people who came to him. The crippled began to walk. The deaf began to hear. Even the blind began to see!

17

One time a young girl had died. When Jesus took her hand and told her to get up, she came back to life!

19

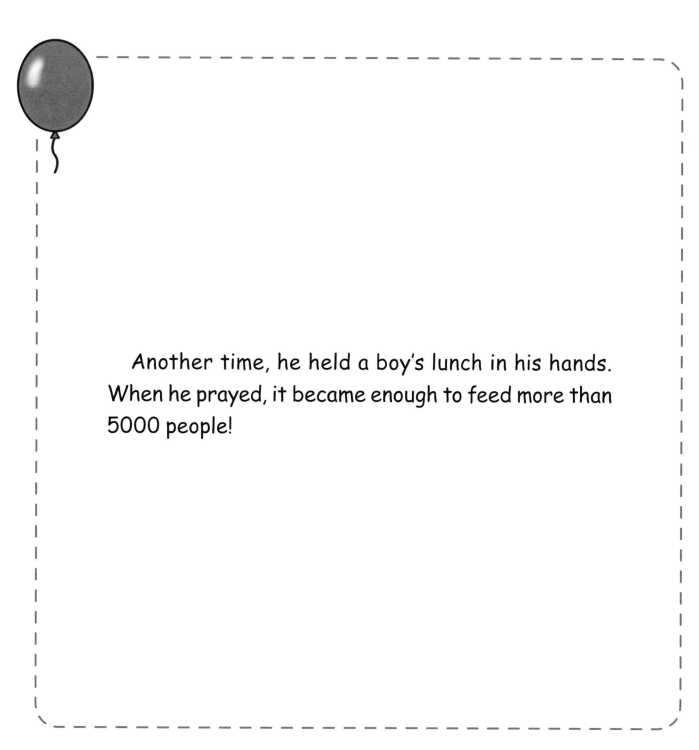

Another time, he held a boy's lunch in his hands. When he prayed, it became enough to feed more than 5000 people!

Jesus did many other great things too, like walking on top of the water and stopping a terrible storm just by telling it to be still.

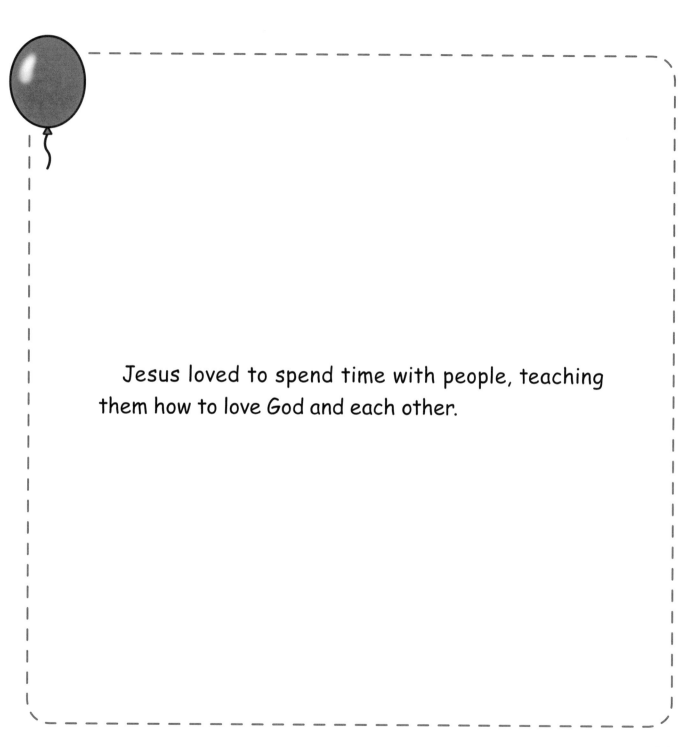

Jesus loved to spend time with people, teaching them how to love God and each other.

But not everyone liked Jesus. Some people did not believe that he was God's Son, so they put him on a wooden cross and killed him. Jesus let them do this to him. He knew that God had a special plan. The friends of Jesus were very sad. They did not understand yet that Jesus was dying for them and for all of us. But why would Jesus die for us?

Jesus knew about the wall of sin. He knew that we could never be with God or go to heaven with sin in our hearts. Jesus died so that his perfect, powerful blood could wash away our sins. Do you see how much Jesus loves us? He gave up his life so that we could go to heaven someday and live in friendship with God, now and forever. He is so wonderful!

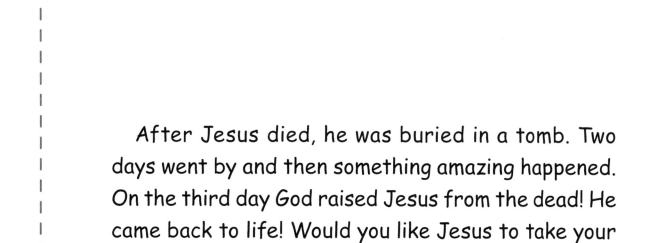

After Jesus died, he was buried in a tomb. Two days went by and then something amazing happened. On the third day God raised Jesus from the dead! He came back to life! Would you like Jesus to take your sins away and be your friend?

The Big Choice

God is waiting for you to choose. Do you want to follow the ways of sin or do you want to follow Jesus? What side do you want to be on?

If you want Jesus to come into your life and take your sins away you can pray a prayer like this: "Lord Jesus, I believe that you are the one true Son of God. Thank you for dying on the cross for my sins. I'm sorry for all the wrong things I've done. Please forgive me. Come into my life, Lord Jesus, and be with me always. Help me to be the person you want me to be. Thank you for answering my prayer, Amen."

If you pray a prayer like this and really mean it,
Jesus will forgive all your sins and come into your life.

You'll begin a great adventure with Jesus and in his word, he promises that he will never leave you. Welcome to the family of God!

Growing in Jesus

God wants you to get to know him better and he wants you to grow strong in his love. How can a little seed grow into a healthy, beautiful tree? It needs lots of good soil, water, air and sunlight. How can you grow stronger in God? Here's what to do:

- Talk to God every day. You can ask him for help in everything and give him thanks.
- Read God's word, the Bible, or ask someone to read it to you. You may want to begin with a children's story Bible.
- Trust and obey God. When you realize that you've sinned, confess it to God. Thank him for forgiving you. Turn away from sin and ask Jesus to fill you with his power to do what's right.
- Meet together with other Christians who teach the Bible and worship Jesus.
- Tell others about Jesus and show them his love.

Printed in the United States
by Baker & Taylor Publisher Services